Applying to College

Applying to College

Casey Watts

A LifeWorks® Guide

Da Capo

LIFE
LONG

A Member of the Perseus Books Group

Library of Congress Control Number: 2003100274
ISBN-13 978-0-7382-0895-4   ISBN-10 0-7382-0895-7

Da Capo Press is a Member of the Perseus Books Group.
Find us on the World Wide Web at http://www.dacapopress.com.

Da Capo Press books are available at special discounts for bulk purchases in the U.S. by corporations, institutions, and other organizations. For more information, please contact the Special Markets Department at the Perseus Books Group, 11 Cambridge Center, Cambridge, MA 02142, or call (800) 255–1514 or (617) 252–5298, or e-mail special.markets@perseusbooks.com.

A word to parents

The purpose of the book is to help your teenager make an informed choice about college—so it's been written specifically for students.

As a parent, you play an important but delicate role in the college selection process. As the awesome task of choosing a college begins, your teenager needs you more than ever. Your son or daughter needs your guidance, wisdom, love, and support. But your teenager also needs you to step back, to let him or her take charge of the college selection process. That's not easy. Choosing a college and going through the admissions process can be a difficult and frustrating experience for both parents and students. There are the pressures of tests, deadlines, essays, and competition. But the college application process can also be a rewarding and expansive learning opportunity that brings you all closer together. The more you know about the process, the more you can help. The more you're willing to listen to your teenager, the more smoothly things will go. Try to keep in mind throughout the next few months or years that it's your son or daughter who is going to college. Try to see things through your teenager's eyes. Explore the possibilities the future holds together and you'll have fun along the way.

Contents

Introduction

If you're in high school, you're probably starting to think about college. You might be asking yourself questions like, "How do I start the college search?" "How will I choose the right school for me?" "What counts most in getting accepted?" These are all important questions. By planning ahead and working together with your parents, teachers, and guidance counselor, the college application process doesn't have to feel overwhelming.

This book can help you think about a strategy for making the right decisions. It will help you organize the entire college application process, from your freshman year to your senior year of high school. Use it as a working tool to help you develop your personal plan. Remember, the more you plan ahead—by thinking about what you want, what your interests are, and what your college options are—the more informed your choice will be.

The college
selection process

College selection worksheet

Choosing a school where you'll feel comfortable and fit in is one of the most important considerations in the selection process. Use this chart as a tool to help you indicate what is important to you in a college.

What's important for you?

	Very important	Somewhat important	Not important
Cost (stipulate range)	◯	◯	◯
Distance from home	◯	◯	◯
College selectivity	◯	◯	◯
Location	◯	◯	◯
Two-year college	◯	◯	◯
Four-year college	◯	◯	◯

	Very important	Somewhat important	Not important
Size of enrollment	O	O	O
Private	O	O	O
Public	O	O	O
Living arrangements	O	O	O
Athletics	O	O	O
Area of studies	O	O	O
Extracurricular activities	O	O	O
Co-op programs	O	O	O
Foreign study	O	O	O
Reputation	O	O	O
Campus life	O	O	O
ROTC	O	O	O
Urban school	O	O	O
Rural campus	O	O	O
Safety	O	O	O

Creating a personal data portfolio

Every college requires you, the applicant, to provide factual information about yourself. Start compiling your personal data now, and fill in information (like SAT scores and extracurricular activities) as it becomes available. Using this form will help you keep the information in one place and make completing individual applications easier later on. In addition, putting certain things down on paper—your school information, activities, community service, and work experience—can reveal to you your strengths, talents, and interests, and how to best match those with a college.

Personal data

Name _____

Address _____

_____

_____

Phone number _____

E-mail _____

Social Security number _____

Parents

Father _____

Mother _____

Mother's maiden name _____

High school

School _____

Address _____

_____

Phone number _____

Guidance counselor _____

CEEB number _____

(This identification number, given to your high school by the College Board, is
available from your guidance counselor. You will need it when applying to college.)

	Freshman	Sophomore	Junior	Senior
Grade Point Average				
Class Rank				
Test Scores				
PSAT/PLAN				
SAT I				
SAT II: Subject Tests				
ACT				

Awards and honors

_____

_____

_____

_____

_____

_____

_____

_____

_____

Extracurricular activities

Sports _____

_____

_____

_____

_____

Clubs _____

_____

_____

_____

_____

Drama _____

_____

_____

_____

_____

Art _____

_____

_____

_____

_____

Music _____

_____

_____

_____

_____

Leadership _____

_____

_____

_____

_____

Volunteer _____

_____

_____

_____

_____

Other _____

_____

_____

_____

_____

_____

_____

Work experience

(List where you have worked, for how long, and what your job responsibilities were. Jot down the name, phone number, and e-mail of anyone who could give you a recommendation.)

_____

_____

_____

_____

_____

_____

_____

Community service

(List where you worked, for how long, and what you did. List the name, phone number, and e-mail of anyone who could give you a solid recommendation.)

_____

_____

_____

_____

_____

_____

_____

Travel

(List any travel or travel-related experiences—such as an
Outward Bound trip or a bike trip—that you feel helped
you grow. Jot down a few sentences about how each
experience contributed to your personal growth.)

_____

_____

_____

_____

_____

_____

Qualities found in the student body

Almost all colleges have a wide variety of students, but you will feel more at home if the mix of students feels comfortable to you. What characteristics would you like to find in other students? What do you value in others? What do you look for in a friend? Circle each quality or trait that you consider important, and write in any other characteristics you would like to find in the student body where you go to college.

ambitious	responsible	diverse
artistic	social	involved
athletic	laid-back	outdoorsy
down-to-earth	liberal	caring
friendly	sophisticated	idealistic
career-oriented	fun	studious
spirited	motivated	independent
competitive	politically aware	tolerant
conservative	progressive	innovative
intellectual	traditional	unpretentious
unconventional	creative	religious
_____	_____	_____
_____	_____	_____

Academic and social atmosphere assessment

While many schools may match your academic profile, it's important to identify the kind of academic and social atmosphere where you will feel most comfortable and successful. Here are some questions to ask yourself. You may want to discuss your responses with your parent or guidance counselor to form a clearer picture of what type of college would be the best choice for you.

- Do you prefer small or large classes?

- Do you work better when the teacher has time to meet with you one-on-one, or do you prefer to work independently?

- Do you want a school with many opportunities for activities, athletics, and leadership?

- Would you rather attend a college with a very intellectual, academic emphasis, or one with a balance between intellectual and social life?

- Do you think you would thrive in a rigorous, high-pressure atmosphere, or would you do better in a school with a more moderate amount of academic pressure?

- Is the option to take many different academic courses important to you? Or would you prefer a more career-directed course load?

- Do you want to attend a college with an emphasis on religious life?

- Are you interested in a single-sex college or a college oriented toward a particular ethnic group?

- Are you looking for a smaller student body, or a larger, more anonymous environment?

- Would you prefer a college in a city, suburb, rural area, or small town?

- Is it important for you to attend a college near your home or in your home state, or are you open to attending college in another region of the country?

- After carefully considering your academic profile, how selective should the colleges you apply to be?

- How important is cost and financial aid availability in making your decision?

Approximately 16.7 million students are enrolled in post-secondary study in the United States. More than half of these students receive some form of financial aid.

The college admissions process

Most students apply to between four and seven schools. The schools are generally a mix of selectivity. Your final list should include some schools that you consider safe to get into, some that are likely possibilities, and a few that are a reach to get into.

When colleges make admission decisions they usually evaluate applicants in three areas:

1. Academic achievement

2. Standardized test scores

3. Personal profile

Academic achievement

Academic achievement is generally the most important criterion. It includes the quality of courses taken, grades, rank in class, and in some cases, teacher recommendations. The quality of courses is determined by academic level, such as general, college preparatory, and honors. Grades and class rank are most important. So don't forget to study hard!

Standardized test scores

The second component is test scores, either SAT I or ACT. At most highly selective colleges, these tests are used in conjunction with the College Board SAT II: Subject Tests.

Most colleges require applicants to take a number of standardized tests and submit their scores. Check the information you have received from the schools you're interested in to find out what tests they require. Some special needs students may qualify for arrangements such as extended time limits or untimed tests. Registration forms and lists of test dates and centers are available in your high school guidance office.

- *For information on the PSAT* contact:
  PSAT/NMSQT Office
  P.O. Box 6720
  Princeton, New Jersey 08541-6720
  609-771-7070
  psat@info.collegeboard.org

- *For information on the SAT* contact:
  College Board SAT Program
  P.O. Box 6200
  Princeton, New Jersey 08541-6200
  609-771-7600
  www.collegeboard.com

- *For information about the PLAN or ACT* contact:
  American College Testing Program
  2201 North Dodge Street
  P.O. Box 168
  Iowa City, Iowa 52243
  319-337-1000
  www.act.org

Some common tests are explained below:

ACT: The American College Testing Program Assessment used to be required primarily by midwestern and southern colleges and universities, but is being accepted by more and more institutions regardless of location. The ACT tests four areas: English, mathematics, reading, and science reasoning. Calculators are not allowed during the math test. The tests are designed to assess educational development and readiness to handle college-level work. Each area is scored separately; a composite score is also given. Many colleges now ask either for the SAT and three SAT II: Subject Tests, or for the ACT.

PLAN: (Formerly PACT): The preliminary version of the American College Testing Program Assessment is given in the 10th grade as practice for the ACT.

PSAT: The Preliminary SAT is a test in four 30-minute sections given in October and April as a practice test to familiarize sophomores and juniors with the SAT I. Results are reported in detail, so strengths and weaknesses can be easily assessed. The junior year PSAT also serves as the only National Merit Scholarship Qualifying Test (NMSQT) for students who may qualify to be designated as National Merit scholars, finalists, semifinalists, or commended students.

SAT I: A three-hour reasoning test given in two sections: verbal and mathematics. The verbal section contains analogies, sentence completion, and critical reading. The math section contains multiple choice, quantitative comparisons, and student-produced responses to questions. Calculators (you must supply your own) are permitted but not required. The SAT I is usually offered at least five times throughout the year. It's best to take the test twice: once in the spring of your junior year, and again in the fall of your senior year. Scaled scores range from 200 to 800 in each section, with an average score of 500 in each section, or 1000 combined. The national SAT average in 2001 was 1020.

SAT II: Subject Tests: Each SAT II is a one-hour test measuring competence in a specific subject. You may take up to three tests on any given date and may decide the order in which to take them. It's generally best to take an SAT II test when you've just completed a course on the test subject. For instance, if you take biology as a junior, take the SAT II in biology in the spring of your junior year.

Note: When you register for an SAT II: Subject Test, you may select the Score Choice option and review your scores before releasing them to colleges or scholarship programs. Once you've received your scores, you can release any or all of them at any time. Once released, however, those particular scores may not be withheld by you again.

TOEFL: The Test of English as a Foreign Language is a standardized exam testing English language skill proficiency, generally taken by students who have learned English as a second language. This test is required by many post-secondary institutions and consists of three sections: Listening Comprehension, Structure and Written Expression, and Vocabulary and Reading Comprehension. For more information, call the Educational Testing Service at 609-771-7100; visit their Web site at www.toefl.org; or e-mail them at toefl@ets.org.

Worth noting

- Test registration deadlines are printed in all registration booklets. Register for each test well before the deadline. If you miss the deadline, there may be late registration or walk-in possibilities. Talk with your guidance counselor or contact the test programs for details. You can register online for most tests.

- Scores will automatically be sent to the colleges to which you are applying if you designate their names on the test registration forms. If you do not fill in those names, you will be responsible for getting the scores to the school(s) at a later date and you will have to pay an extra fee to do so. (Scores are also listed on your high school transcript, so it might be possible to avoid paying extra fees.)

- PSAT and SAT scores may seem higher now compared to a few years ago because of re-centering, a change in the test scoring system that took place after the 1994-95 academic year. The Educational Testing Service, which administers the tests, has artificially raised combined scores by about 100 points. Average PSAT/SAT scores in the math and verbal sections are now 500, with a combined average score of 1000. This will have very little effect on college applications, since colleges will adjust their expectations accordingly. For example, a school that previously looked for a combined score of 890 will now be looking for a score of 1000.

- To prep or not to prep? That is the question and it's a big one. There is serious debate as to whether prepping for these tests helps to raise scores, though common sense dictates that establishing familiarity with a test is likely to be helpful. Two recent studies from the College Board showed that "students taking out-of-school coaching were likely to experience an average gain of 6 to 12 points on the verbal score and 13 to 26 points on the math score." In other words, tutoring can raise scores, but not significantly. Many schools offer classes in test preparation, and private courses and tutoring are usually available. A number of prep books and computer software programs can also be quite helpful. The decision to prep is an individual one. If you choose to do so, remember that to succeed you must be committed to putting time into studying.

Early action - An admissions plan that allows you to apply before the normal deadline and receive the college's decision in advance of regular applicants. If you are admitted on this plan, you do not have to accept until May 1 and may still apply to other colleges.

Early decision - An admissions plan that allows you to apply before the normal deadline (usually in November or December) and receive the college's decision within a short time. If you are accepted on this plan, you are obligated to enroll at the college and must withdraw any other applications.

Personal profile

The third component, the personal profile, measures what the candidate does outside the classroom. This profile includes jobs, athletics, community service, religious activities, extracurricular activities, and more. Unlike test scores and academic achievement, which are relatively easy to measure, the personal profile is far more difficult to evaluate. The application and letters of recommendation are two ways in which colleges gather information in this area. Some colleges use a personal interview with a student, which is another way for the college to evaluate a student's personal profile.

The relative weight given to each of these elements in the college's decision-making varies greatly. Large public universities are less likely to use the personal profile and are more apt to use test scores, formulas, and GPA or class rank cut-offs than are smaller, private colleges. In most cases, weaknesses in one area can be offset by strengths in another. Remember, the more selective a college, the more that college expects high academic achievement, test scores, and a favorable personal profile.

Keep in mind that colleges have other priorities that affect student admission, such as ethnic or cultural mix, geographical mix, talent mix, need for athletes, and general diversity of student body.

The college application

The application is a crucial document in the admissions process. It demonstrates the quality of your writing and thinking, and tells the college how you've spent your time. Your application should be well-written and thoughtful. Regardless of how good your grades are, a poorly written, careless application can hurt your chances of acceptance. Unfortunately, there is no sure-fire formula that will guarantee a good application. But you may want to keep the following tips in mind:

- Read through all the materials received before filling in any information on the application. Make extra copies for practice.

- Follow directions carefully.

- Be aware of deadlines and allow yourself plenty of time to develop a strong application. Be sure to request transcripts and recommendations so they arrive on time.

- Revise and rewrite it, leave it "on the shelf" for a few days, and then review it. Have a teacher, friend, or parent review it, too.

- Type the application or neatly print in black or blue ink.

- Make sure the final application is neat and clean and free of errors. Double check that all applicant sections have been completed. Keep copies of every application you send.

Check to see if the schools you're interested in accept the "Common Application," a single application accepted by a growing number of schools. You can pick up a copy at your high school guidance office, have the college's admission office send you an application, or download a copy from www.commonapp.org.

Online applications

Today, more and more colleges are accepting online applications. Organizations like the College Board offer this type of service for little or no fee. Check out their Web site at www.collegeboard.com for more information.

You should also keep in mind that many colleges have their own Web sites that offer the option of applying online. You simply download and print the application. Remember, it is still important for you to take the time to complete the application carefully and be sure to have others review it.

The college essay

Of all the pieces that make up your college application, the essay can be the most challenging. But it is also a chance to show who you truly are, so the effort is worth it. A well-written, interesting essay can tip the scale in your favor in the admissions process. Remember— while it's probably too late to change grades or test scores, you can always write a better essay if you plan ahead and work at it.

When considering what to write about, think of your college essay as an opportunity to showcase yourself. It is your chance to offer opinions and feelings, and to demonstrate a sense of style that may not be found elsewhere in your application. Expressing creativity is fundamental to a successful essay. Clarity in your self-expression is paramount in revealing what is unique about yourself. Write about you, not what you think the admissions committee wants to hear.

Be prepared to go through several drafts, and even to change your topic several times. Give yourself plenty of time to brainstorm, to revise, and to end up with a finished piece that you're proud of, and that gives the admissions officers a glimpse of who you really are.

Simply put, the typical admissions committee reader is looking at your finished product on three levels:

1. **Command.** Do you demonstrate a command of the English language? Your spelling, grammar, and syntax must all be perfect. Be sure to have others edit your work.

2. **Content.** Do you logically express an idea or argument? Are you able to say something of substance in the given number of words? (Long, drawn-out essays are often penalized.) When finished with each draft, read it aloud. Does the first sentence grab your attention? Does the conclusion leave you with a clear solution or response to the subject? Does this essay reflect who you are?

3. **Creativity.** Creative essays must reflect your individuality. You might express yourself in the form of a story, a brief dialogue, or even with humor. Just be sure to answer what is being asked of you in each application's essay question. For example, writing poetry may certainly be appropriate for an open-ended question, but may prove awkward if the question is specific.

Letters of recommendation

You will be asked to submit letters of recommendation with your application—from a teacher, coach, religious leader, or other community member who knows you well. When choosing whom to ask to write your recommendation, consider teachers who know you and who will take the time to write a meaningful assessment of your performance. Additional recommendations should come from others who also know you well and can provide insight into your leadership skills, character, and abilities. Recommendation letters need to tell something about you that the school is not going to find in your application. Make sure you find out if special forms are required. You should include stamped, addressed envelopes with the recommendation forms so they can be mailed directly to the college. You are the one responsible for making sure the letters of recommendation are written and mailed on time.

The college visit

Most students begin formally visiting colleges in the summer before and the fall of their senior year, but campus visits can really take place any time during your high school years. Keep in mind that if you visit colleges in the summer, the atmosphere might be very different from the school year when most students are there. Also, small things like the weather or an unfriendly tour guide can easily taint your opinion of a school. Before you cross a school off your list because of a rainy day, however, make an effort to learn as much as you can about the school and the student body.

- If the school doesn't offer guided tours, ask if you can simply walk around campus. Find out if there is a fall Open House program or other upcoming on-campus events you can attend.

- Unless you're positive about the kind of school you want to attend, check out several different types— three or so should give you some basis for comparison. It's a good idea to visit a large university (more than 10,000 students), a medium-sized college or university (3,000 to 10,000 students), and a small college (under 3,000 students) to compare. You may also want to look at schools in different locations— cities and small towns, close to home and far away.

- For schools that require them, on-campus interviews can be scheduled for the same day you're visiting. If a group interview or information session is offered, these also can be done the same day as the visit.

Planning your visits

- Talk with your family about how best to schedule the visits and handle transportation. Would a family member like to accompany you to the school? If not, how will you get there? Is a friend's family planning a drive to one of the schools? Is the school accessible by public transportation? If you're traveling for a weekend visit, can an admissions staff member or athletic coach meet you at an airport, train station, or bus stop?

- Call the admissions office a few weeks in advance to find out when they offer tours.

- If you're setting up an on-campus interview, it's wise to call as far ahead as possible—as many as eight weeks in advance for some schools, maybe more in the popular fall months.

- Be sure to ask for directions to campus, places to stay if you'll be there overnight, and how long you might anticipate being on campus (for most schools, plan on at least two hours).

- If your visit happens around a mealtime, ask about meal options on campus (to try the cafeteria food).

- If your visit is over a weekend or you're coming from a distance, ask if you can stay on campus with a current student acting as your host. Some schools offer formal overnight visits, where students stay on campus, eat in the dining hall, and sit in on classes. At other schools, it's done informally on a case-by-case basis.

- Ask the admissions office if you can sit in on a class in your potential major during your visit. If that's not feasible, see if you can speak with a faculty member or with a current student from your potential major while you're on campus.

- If you're interested in specific activities such as sports or organizations, make appointments to speak with coaches, advisers, or leaders.

- If you don't already have information about the school, request an information packet now. Before you go, read it through to familiarize yourself with what the school is saying about itself. Develop a list of questions the information didn't address and bring it with you to the visit.

- Create a "Visit Notebook" or folder to bring with you. In it you can note questions you'd like to ask and your impressions of the school. This record-keeping becomes increasingly important if you visit several schools; they can all start to look alike. If you have a camera, you might find that taking photos of the campus is helpful in jogging your memory later.

- Ask your high school guidance counselor or the college admissions office if they can refer you to graduates of your high school who are currently enrolled at the college you're planning to visit. It could be helpful to talk with them about their experiences—either before or during your visit.

During the visit

- Write the name of your tour guides in your Visit Notebook. (Most tours are conducted by current students.) Ask if they'd mind if you call or write to them after the tour with additional questions. While they are walking around with you, ask questions about their college experience. What are their majors? How did they choose this college? What do they like best about the school? What is the food really like? What is the campus like on weekends? These are questions you might feel awkward asking an admissions representative, but would feel comfortable asking a person closer to your own age.

- If it's convenient, write down answers to important questions in your Visit Notebook. Jot down your impressions of the campus, the dormitories, the classrooms, the people, the library, and the dining hall as soon after the tour as possible.

- As you're touring the school, look at bulletin boards and posters hung up around campus. They can tell you a lot about regular activities, student interests, and special events.

- If the tour doesn't include the library, make sure you visit it on your own. Is it a comfortable place to study? Is it empty or full of students? Does it have current and up-to-date publications? Does it offer an inter-library loan program? Can you access the Internet there? Ask the library staff a little bit about the library—what's new or noteworthy?

- Ask for campus safety information from the admissions office. Schools are required by law to provide statistics of crime on campus to prospective students. If anything concerns you, ask the admissions staff for clarification.

After the visit

- If you have your tour guide's name, and feel comfortable doing so, follow up with him or her. Write a thank you note (c/o the admissions office). If you spoke with other students, a coach, or a faculty member, and feel comfortable doing so, write a follow-up note thanking them for their time.

- Expand on the preliminary thoughts you jotted down in your Visit Notebook. Follow up on any new or unanswered questions with the admissions office. Ask anyone who accompanied you on the tour what their impressions were and how they felt about the school, and note that in your notebook, too.

- If you feel you'd like to apply to a school, ask the admissions office for an application packet (if you don't already have one).

The interview

An integral but often misunderstood part of a college visit is the interview. Schools may use either a group meeting or a personal interview. Many colleges offer both, but appointments for personal interviews may require several weeks' notice. If you can't arrange an on-campus interview, ask if and when a representative from the college will be visiting your high school or area. Many colleges will arrange for you to be interviewed near your home by a local alumnus. If all else fails, interviews may also be conducted over the phone.

A group meeting usually requires little advance notice. This may be set up by the admissions office of the college, a high school guidance counselor, or by you. These are information sessions at which admissions staff members provide you and your parents with a short descriptive talk on the college and an opportunity to ask questions.

In addition to providing information, the personal interview involves an evaluation of the student. The importance of the evaluation will vary from college to college. The personal interview may have a bigger impact at schools that have more selective admissions policies. It may also be used to determine scholarships. Some colleges design interviews to be information-gathering sessions for prospective freshmen.

Most admissions officers do not want parents to sit in on the personal interview. Discuss this ahead of time with your parents; perhaps they can use the interview time to meet with the financial aid office or tour the campus.

Before a college interview

- Find out as much as you can about the college. Read any and all materials you've received; watch the video if you have it; visit the college's Web site. Check your local library or guidance office for guidebooks or computer programs that can tell you more. Talk about the school with your guidance counselor, friends, recent graduates, and parents, and get their opinions.

- Review your high school transcript and think about your extracurricular and summer activities so you can talk about them in depth. Be prepared to discuss your grades and academic record—what you're proud of and what you're not so proud of—if the admissions representative asks you about them.

- Practice answering questions you think an admissions interviewer might ask. Likely questions include the following: Why do you want to go here? What first brought our school to your attention? What do you want to do with your degree and your life? Ask a friend, parent, or another adult to conduct a mock interview, asking questions like these so you can hear how your answers sound. Have them give you the question you'd least want to answer or the question that scares you the most—for example, if there is a grade you're not proud of—and practice what you'd say.

- Think of several questions you would like answered. Every interviewer gives you a chance to ask questions, usually at the end of the interview. Make a list so you don't forget them (and so you look prepared). Avoid basic questions that could be answered in the catalog or guidebook, but be sure to ask about your individual concerns and interests. It can also be helpful to ask for more specifics on the major you're interested in, upcoming events on campus, or scholarship possibilities at the school. If the interview is being held on campus, it might be helpful for you to take your tour beforehand—you'll have time to get an impression of the school, and you may feel more knowledgeable asking specific questions of the admissions representative.

- On the day of the interview, try to be as relaxed and rested as possible. Students typically "dress up" for college interviews. While it's not necessary to purchase a new suit or dress, it is important to look neat and presentable. (Don't wear jeans, for example.)

Wear comfortable shoes if you'll be taking a tour of campus. Be sure to be prompt for the interview, and not more than 10 to 15 minutes early. If you are running late and know you will not be on time, call the admissions office to let them know.

During the interview

- Walk in prepared to have an enjoyable conversation. Admissions representatives are generally pleasant people who are interested in learning more about you. You'll enjoy the interview more and find it easier to present yourself in a favorable way if you walk in with a positive attitude. Remember that the admissions interview is a time when you need to talk; if you're normally a shy or quiet person, try to put that aside for the brief time you're being interviewed.

- In most interviews, you'll be asked about your academic record, your extracurricular activities, and your summer activities. The interviewer will want to go beyond the facts on your application or high school record, so be prepared to discuss what you've done. Don't assume that the interviewer has seen or is familiar with your application or transcript; you may need to remember specific courses you've taken and grades you've received.

- Try to have a thoughtful conversation. An interview should feel more like a discussion than a quiz. Be yourself. Ask questions. If there is something particularly important or unusual about your record, such as a noticeable improvement or decline in your grades, or a particularly interesting course or activity, make sure to bring it up so you'll have a chance to explain it in your own words.

- Sell yourself. This may be the only chance to tell a college what makes you special and what you can contribute to the school.

- It's OK for you to take notes in your Visit Notebook during your interview. You'll be getting a lot of important information from your interviewer that you may want to refer to at a later time.

- If the admissions representative offers you a business card, take it, or be sure to ask for and write down his or her full name and title in your Notebook.

After the interview

- Write a short thank you note to your admissions interviewer. Beyond the common courtesy, it will reinforce the fact that you are interested in the school, and may help you stand out among applicants.

- If you've thought of additional questions since the interview, make a list of them and call the interviewer or admissions office for more information. At some schools, you might also be able to e-mail your questions to the admissions interviewer. Remember, the admissions staff is there to be a resource for you.

Common questions asked at college interviews

- Why are you interested in this college?

- What are you interested in studying at this college?

- What are your strengths?

- What are your weaknesses?

- What do you do in your spare time?

- What kinds of work experiences have you had?

- Who is your favorite author? Why?

- What do you imagine doing ten years from now?

- What extracurricular activities have you participated in?

- In what ways have you served your community?

- If you could change one thing in the world, what would it be?

Sample questions you could ask during the interview

- What campus issues are most important to students?

- What is the strongest academic program at the college?

- What is the most popular department on campus? The most popular course?

- What is the most difficult course, according to students?

- How is the college trying to improve itself?

- How many introductory courses are taught by faculty members and how many are taught by graduate assistants?

- What are the student graduation rates? (The Student Right-to-Know Act requires colleges to monitor and calculate completion and transfer-out rates and to make this information available to current and prospective students.)

- How has this college changed in the last five years?

College admissions timetable

Some students begin planning for college the moment they enter high school freshman year. Others don't start actively planning until well into their junior year. This timetable is meant to be adapted to your needs and what's possible for you.

Grade 9 - freshman year

There isn't much you need to do freshman year to plan for college, except take the most challenging courses you can, and do the best you can in school. With the help of your school's guidance office, you might create a tentative four-year high school plan. If you plan to attend college, your course plan should include the following:

☐ **Math:** Taking the appropriate math courses throughout your high school years will keep your career options open. The minimum requirements for most colleges usually include three years of math, including Algebra I and II and Geometry. If you are able, take Advanced Algebra, Trigonometry, Pre-calculus, or Calculus. Keep in mind that if you plan to major in sciences or engineering in college, you must take senior year math in high school.

☐ **English/Language Arts:** Colleges require four years of English, including both composition and literature. (Fortunately, this is also a requirement for high school graduation.) If you enjoy language arts and have the opportunity to take electives, you might want to take advantage of any honors courses. Make sure they fulfill the college prep criteria.

☐ **Science:** Most colleges require at least two years of high school science. Courses with lab experience, like Biology, Physics, and Chemistry, are typically required. Course work in other sciences, such as Anatomy and Physiology or Biochemistry, will provide you with additional options.

☐ **Social Sciences:** Colleges expect a minimum of two years of study in Social Sciences or History. (As with English/Language Arts, these two years will also satisfy the minimum high school graduation requirement.) If you have the interest and available options at your school, however, you should consider taking more.

☐ **Foreign Language:** Most colleges look for a minimum of two years of study in a single foreign language and prefer more. Students who cannot meet this requirement for reasons such as a serious learning disability may be offered alternative programs and opportunities. It is more advantageous to focus on a single language and not to jump from one to another each year. As with math, insufficient foreign language preparation can limit your college choices. Advanced work will allow you to consider colleges requiring more than the two-year minimum in foreign language study.

Grade 10 - sophomore year

Fall

☐ Take a careful look at your extracurricular activities. Is your list of activities well rounded, or does it mostly focus on one specific area? Do you need to consider adding some different activities to your roster?

☐ Review your course of study with your guidance office, and fine-tune it if necessary. Are you on track with college preparatory classes, and are you taking the most challenging level of classes for your capabilities?

☐ Begin to become acquainted with the college resources available in your guidance office. Is there a college video library for students to use? A collection of college books you can look at? Is there a computer you can use? Are there practice tests for the PSAT and PLAN? Is there a schedule posted of when college representatives will be visiting your school?

Spring

☐ Register for any SAT II: Subject Tests or AP (Advanced Placement) tests in subjects you'll complete this year, for example, Biology or Chemistry. It's generally best to take these tests when you've just completed a course on the test subject.

☐ Talk with athletic coaches about NCAA (National Collegiate Athletic Association) requirements, recruiting guidelines, and regulations. Order the NCAA Clearinghouse Manual through your athletic department, or by calling 800-638-3731.

Grade 11 - junior year

Fall

☐ Obtain a Social Security number for use on college applications, if you don't already have one. Your parents can help you with this. (Look in the phone book's government or business section for the Social Security Administration office nearest you.)

☐ Register for the PSAT/NMSQT (Preliminary SAT/ National Merit Scholarship Qualifying Test) through your guidance office. Typically, registration is in October. (The test itself is given twice a year—in October and April.) Take the practice test found inside the free PSAT bulletin available in your guidance office. The junior year PSAT serves as the only qualifying test for students who might be National Merit scholars, finalists, semi-finalists, or commended students.

☐ Review the courses and extracurricular activities you're taking this year. Is the course work challenging enough? Is it possible to move up a level to an honors or AP class? (Colleges typically weigh these classes more heavily in your academic average.) What about extracurricular activities—are your activities well rounded? If you still haven't become involved with any group, try at least one activity this year.

Spring

☐ Begin reviewing an SAT preparation book for 15 minutes per night. These books can be purchased from a bookstore or borrowed from the library.

☐ Review your PSAT scores as well as the section that details your incorrect responses and the correct answers.

☐ Register for the spring SAT I, SAT II, and ACT as necessary.

☐ Determine which colleges you're most interested in visiting. If the campus is far from home, check with your guidance office to see if it has that school's video, or call the school and request a video. Many schools have videos available on their Internet home pages. Reviewing these videos can give you a preliminary idea of what the school looks like. If you're still interested and willing to make the trip, you've done some legwork beforehand that didn't cost you anything.

☐ Begin working on a résumé to present to the teachers whom you ask for recommendations. Think about choosing a teacher who has written detailed (positive!) comments on your work. It's a good idea to schedule time to talk with this teacher; he will have a lot more to write about if he knows more about you. You don't want a vague recommendation. Give your teacher a page that includes your name, address, grade point average to date, any honors you've received, extracurricular activities, clubs, and sports you participate in. List information on a job you currently have, and anything else you can think of. Share literature from the college's admissions office with your teacher, so he can gear comments toward what the school says it's looking for. Use the "personal data portfolio" to help you compile your résumé.

☐ Find out if schools you're interested in accept the Common Application. Information about the Common Application should be available in your guidance office, from the college itself, or online at www.commonapp.org.

☐ Use the Internet as you gather information about colleges. Increasing numbers of schools are creating Web sites for potential students' use. You can often request material about a college online. Some schools also offer you the option of e-mailing questions to the school, which will be answered by current students, the admissions office, and faculty members. A growing number of sites also offer information about financial aid and how to search for scholarships and loans.

☐ Begin to research scholarships. Remember that there are scholarships based on financial need as well as merit scholarships. Look at scholarship books in your local library or guidance office. Use the Internet to explore options. Call your state's Higher Education Agency for help—your guidance counselor should have this phone number. Find out if either of your parents' employers offers scholarships to college-bound students. If you've had a part-time job during high school, ask if that employer has scholarships. If you've ever delivered newspapers, bagged groceries, volunteered at a local organization, or if you attend a church, synagogue, or other establishment, see if it offers college scholarships. Most scholarships are locally based. All students should also submit the Free Application for Federal Student Aid (FAFSA).

☐ If you are applying for early decision at any college, make sure you have taken all required tests prior to the close of junior year.

☐ By the end of junior year, you should be contacting schools to request brochures, college view books, and information about campus tours and Open House programs. Generally, application forms for the upcoming year are not available until the end of the summer. You may be able to get information from schools using the Internet.

☐ Make appointments to visit campuses by calling the school's admissions office. Be sure to ask if the school requires an interview; you could schedule that interview during your visit.

Grade 12 - senior year

Summer

☐ You should begin to narrow your list to colleges of greatest interest. Most students apply to between four and seven schools.

☐ Keep a planning calendar close by with all of your deadlines, test dates, appointments for campus visits and interviews, admission deadlines, financial aid deadlines, and so forth.

Fall

☐ Write down the final list of colleges to which you are applying.

☐ If your first SAT I/ACT scores were low, take the November/December tests and forward scores to the colleges to which you are applying.

☐ Most early action and early decision applications are due November 1-15. Make sure all application materials are forwarded to the college well in advance of the deadline date if early decision is your choice.

☐ Ask teachers and counselors if they're willing to write letters of recommendation for your college applications. Indicate which schools you're thinking about, tell them what your summer plans are (if you know), and let them know when you expect to be able to give them the recommendation form. (Remember to write a brief note of thanks when the recommendation letters are done.)

☐ Concentrate on keeping up your grades as you close in on the home stretch of the application process. Remember, many colleges will see your first semester grades and will be impressed if you've taken challenging courses.

☐ Register for the ACT, SAT I, and SAT II, as necessary. (For instance, the SAT I is usually offered five times throughout the year.)

☐ Wrap up campus visits, and, if you want to, schedule a time to spend an overnight at the college(s) you're most interested in.

☐ Investigate the fall visiting schedule of college representatives, which your guidance office will have. Schedule appointments with reps from any schools that particularly interest you. These appointments can serve as an ideal time to work on your interviewing skills.

☐ Continue to work on essay drafts and have someone edit and proofread your efforts.

☐ Meet with your counselor to review your final list of schools. Review how your guidance office will be involved in the processing of college applications. Determine how your college applications will be sent.

☐ If you're an athlete and wish to compete in Division I or II college athletics as a freshman, you must register and be certified by the NCAA Initial-Eligibility Clearinghouse. Your high school counselor should provide you with a student release form and a brochure entitled "Making Sure You Are Eligible to Participate in College Sports." Although you may register at any time before senior year, it's ideal to register with the NCAA Clearinghouse after your junior year grades appear on your transcript.

More than 50 percent of all college students do not graduate from the college where they started!

Senior year monthly strategy

This month-by-month checklist will help you stay on track and pay careful attention to deadlines. Being late, even by one day, can mean the difference between an acceptance or rejection of your admissions or financial aid application.

Goals for October

☐ Review for any standardized tests you'll be taking.

☐ Pick up the CSS/Financial Aid PROFILE form from your guidance office.

☐ Familiarize yourself with the exact process by which transcripts and applications are mailed.

☐ Photocopy all application forms before you fill them out, and use the duplicate as a worksheet.

☐ Have your counselor, English teacher, or parent check your college application essays.

☐ Mail early decision or action applications after carefully checking them and making duplicate copies of the final applications for your files. Many students send their applications by registered mail, which provides a tracking number and requires a signature upon delivery.

☐ Take the appropriate October tests you've already registered for.

Other tasks:

_____

_____

_____

_____

_____

_____

_____

_____

Goals for November

☐ Be sure you've filled out the necessary forms ensuring that ACT, SAT I, and SAT II: Subject Test scores will be sent to your colleges of choice.

☐ Double check that the people who agreed to write your recommendations have the appropriate forms, stamped envelopes, and reminders about the due dates.

☐ Confirm that your transcript has been sent to your colleges of choice.

☐ Complete all remaining applications, making copies of everything. File copies accordingly in a designated spot at home.

☐ Inquire about any overnight programs being offered at the colleges you're interested in.

☐ Write and mail thank you notes to everyone who wrote a letter of recommendation.

Other tasks:

_____

_____

_____

_____

_____

Goals for December

☐ Take any necessary ACT, SAT I, and SAT II tests.

☐ Verify with your counselor that all applications, transcripts, and test scores are out to prospective colleges. (Complete any unfinished applications, making copies for your home files.)

☐ Check with the colleges you're applying to and find out which financial aid forms they require.

☐ Pick up the Free Application for Federal Student Aid (FAFSA) at your school's guidance office.

Other tasks:

_____

_____

_____

_____

_____

_____

_____

_____

Goals for January

☐ Complete applications for those colleges with later deadlines or rolling admissions.

☐ Prepare all the required financial aid forms.

☐ Check with the colleges' admissions offices to verify they have received all required materials from you and your high school.

Other tasks:

_____

_____

_____

_____

_____

_____

_____

Goals for February

☐ Confirm that your mid-year report goes to every college to which you've applied.

☐ Send in all of your financial aid forms, after making copies for your personal files.

☐ Write to let colleges know of any new honors or accomplishments you've achieved.

Other tasks:

_____

_____

_____

_____

_____

_____

_____

_____

Goals for March

☐ Register for any Advanced Placement test(s) you want to take later in the spring.

☐ Watch the mail for your Student Aid Report from the federal government. Respond immediately if any changes or corrections are necessary.

☐ Call the Financial Aid office at colleges where you have applied to determine if they require any additional information.

☐ If applying to colleges with rolling admissions, complete those applications by the end of the month to ensure eligibility for any financial aid programs.

☐ Check with your guidance counselor and other local resources for grant or local scholarship opportunities.

Other tasks:

_____

_____

_____

_____

_____

_____

_____

Goals for April

☐ Review the acceptances and financial aid offers you receive with family and your guidance counselor.

☐ Be sure you understand the financial aid offer. Call or write to the school(s) if you want to reject their offer at this time.

☐ Go back to visit your top-choice schools, then make your final decision.

☐ Be sure the school you've chosen receives your deposit by its deadline.

Other tasks:

_____

_____

_____

_____

_____

_____

_____

_____

Goals for May

☐ Take AP exams.

☐ Continue to explore any financial assistance opportunities in your community.

☐ If registered with the NCAA, verify that all paperwork is up-to-date in preparation for your upcoming freshman year.

Other tasks:

_____

_____

_____

_____

_____

_____

_____

Goals for the summer

☐ Complete any outstanding financial aid paperwork.

☐ Find out from your college if you'll have roommates.

☐ Contact your roommates to find out who will bring what. For example, who will bring the phone? The stereo?

☐ Relax, visit with friends, earn some extra spending money at your summer job, and look forward to your first year in college!

Other tasks:

_____

_____

_____

_____

_____

_____

_____

_____

Financial aid basics
(for parents)

Financial aid fills the gap between the cost of college attendance—tuition fees, books and supplies, room and board, and personal expenses—and what your family can afford to pay. There are three main types of aid:

- **Grants and scholarships.** These awards do not have to be paid back.

- **Loans.** Loans are borrowed by the student or parent and must be repaid at a later time.

- **Federal work-study.** Student employment, sometimes called work-study, allows students to earn money for books or other educational costs while going to school.

Expected Family Contribution (EFC) is the amount your family is expected to contribute toward your child's education. This is the number that's used in determining your child's eligibility for federal student aid.

Grants and scholarships

Grants are usually need-based and are awarded to students who have demonstrated the greatest financial need. Because federal grant money is limited, it's important to apply early.

- **Pell Grants.** When you fill out the FAFSA, you are also applying for the Federal Pell Grant Program, which is the largest source of need-based grant money. The grants are awarded to undergraduate students who demonstrate the greatest financial need.

- **Federal Supplemental Educational Opportunity Grants (FSEOG).** College financial aid offices offer this grant to its students who demonstrate the most financial need, usually Pell Grant recipients.

Scholarships are essentially merit-based grants. They are awarded based on a student's special skills or achievement. Scholarships are available from a variety of places, including foundations, nonprofit organizations, corporations, federal and state governments, and even some colleges.

- Check with your teenager's high school guidance department to find out about community-based scholarships from local businesses, civic organizations, or community groups.

- Your local library may have books that list national scholarships. If your teenager is interested in a specific field of study, your librarian can help you identify and locate information on professional associations in that field.

- Call your state's higher education agency. Many states give college money to students with specific interests and needs. Some states, for example, provide scholarship funds to students who are willing to make a commitment to teach in a public school.

- Online scholarship search sites such as www.fastweb.com can be a fast way to find information about thousands of scholarship opportunities.

- If you are a veteran, explore what's available through veterans' organizations, or at www.gibill.va.gov.

- Check with your employer to see if your organization offers scholarships to children of employees.

It can take time to do the research, but a few phone calls and letters, or an afternoon at the library, just might turn up a scholarship that makes your child's college education more affordable.

Loans

Many families borrow money to finance a child's college education. Loans are available through the federal government, privately through many banks, and through other lending institutions. Here are some loan options to consider:

- **Federal Perkins Loan.** This loan is a low-interest (5 percent) loan guaranteed by the government and granted by colleges to students with the most financial need. Interest does not accrue until the student is no longer in school and repayment begins nine months after graduation.

- **Subsidized/Unsubsidized Federal Stafford Loan.** Stafford Loans are guaranteed by the federal government. The interest rate is capped at 8.25 percent. Your child can borrow from $2,625 to $5,500 a year, depending on what year of school your child is in;

she may borrow for as long as she is enrolled in school at least part time. Repayment begins six months after your child graduates. Stafford Loan applications are available from college financial aid offices.

- **Federal Parent PLUS Loan.** PLUS loans are also backed by the federal government, and the interest rate is capped at 9 percent. Parents, not students, borrow the money. The yearly limit on a PLUS loan is equal to the total cost of attendance minus other financial aid. Loan repayment begins 30 to 45 days after the loan is made. PLUS loan applications are available from college financial aid offices.

- **Home equity lines of credit.** If you are a property owner, you might consider using a home equity loan to pay for education costs. The interest is tax-deductible. Check with your bank to find out about current interest rates.

Federal work-study

This federal need-based program allows students to earn money from the school by working at a subsidized job, generally on the college campus. Ask the college financial aid office for more information about work-study opportunities.

Sample financial aid packages

A financial aid package is the total amount of money a college offers a student. Packages may differ from school to school, and are based on a family's ability to pay, the school's financial aid resources, and other factors.

Here are three sample packages for the same student at three different schools:

- **Package 1 — "meet full need" package at a private college.** A "meet full need" financial aid package covers all expenses, including tuition and room and board, minus the Expected Family Contribution (EFC). It might include a combination of loans, grants, and work-study money. For example, if the cost of attendance is $22,500 and the EFC is $8,000, the amount of financial need is $14,500. In this case, the package might include a Stafford Loan of $2,625, which the student would have to repay; federal work-study money totaling $875 (this is money the student earns at an on-campus job); and a college grant of $11,000, which would not have to be repaid. If the family chose to borrow money to help pay the EFC, they could do so using other loan sources. If the student also received an outside scholarship of $2,500 (from the parent's employer, for example), that amount would most likely be added to the college aid package, and not to the EFC.

The family's cost at this school would be $8,000.

- **Package 2 — federal loan and outside scholarship money at a state school.** In this example, the cost of attendance at the school the student is considering is much lower—$7,900. He would not be eligible for financial aid because his EFC equals the cost of attendance. But the student could still take out a Stafford Loan of $2,625 and still receive an outside scholarship of $2,500, if eligible.

The family's cost at this school would be $2,775.

- **Package 3 — federal loan and outside scholarship money at a private college.** At the third school the student is considering, the cost of attendance is $19,500. But the school has limited financial resources and does not offer scholarship or grant money. The student could still take out a Stafford Loan of $2,625, and still receive an outside scholarship of $2,500, if eligible.

The family's cost at this school would be $14,375.

College financing
timetable (for parents)

Keeping track of financial aid forms and deadlines can be tricky. Use the checklist on the following pages to help make sure you meet all the deadlines.

Don't forget

1. File for financial aid at each college where your teenager applies.

2. You must file a separate financial aid form for each child you have in college.

3. You should discuss any special circumstances with a college financial aid officer.

4. You must re-apply for financial aid yearly.

Grade 11 - junior year

Fall

☐ Get copies of the financial aid forms—the Free Application for Federal Student Aid (FAFSA) and the CSS/Financial Aid profile are most common—from your teenager's school counselor, the college financial aid office, banks, or libraries, or contact the higher education agency in your state. You can also visit www.fafsa.ed.gov. Check with your son or daughter's guidance counselor to see if any state or federal regulations have changed.

☐ Attend a financial aid information night at your teenager's high school or at a nearby college to learn about the process. Practice filling out the FAFSA to see if you understand the questions and have all of the information required.

Spring

☐ Pick up information on financial aid policies at local colleges. If there are none nearby, write, e-mail, or call a college for copies. Most colleges will have brochures describing how financial aid is awarded. Use this to plan for your needs.

Grade 12 - senior year

Fall

☐ Pick up copies of the financial aid forms if you haven't already. Be sure you have the correct forms for the right colleges. Many colleges have a form of their own instead of, or in addition to, the FAFSA or PROFILE forms. Forms are usually available in November.

☐ Apply for a Personal Identification Number (PIN) if you'll be completing the FAFSA online. You'll need a PIN number in order to electronically sign your application, and obtaining one can take two weeks or more.

☐ If you need to search for additional funds to pay for college, check with your teenager's guidance counselor about local or national scholarships. Check with the financial aid officer of the colleges to which your son or daughter is applying, too.

☐ File the FAFSA and PROFILE forms as soon after January 1 as possible. Always try to file by February 15. The sooner you file, the better your chance of being considered for limited funds.

☐ . You do not need to have completed current income tax forms. Estimates of last year's earnings will do, although as soon as you file completed copies of your taxes, it may be necessary to mail a copy to the colleges handling your financial aid processing.

☐ It is most important that you follow the instructions on the forms exactly. Errors, omissions, or failing to follow directions will create costly delays for you. Don't forget to include a check for the proper amount to cover any processing fees. And make copies of everything submitted!

Spring

☐ When your financial aid form has been processed at the central processing center you will receive a Student Aid Report (SAR) and acknowledgment page. Make sure the information is correct and was sent to the colleges to which your teenager is applying. If there are any errors, make the corrections on that page and return it immediately.

☐ The SAR will tell you about your eligibility for financial aid and your Expected Family Contribution (EFC). Save the SAR. You may need it.

☐ Make sure you complete any other applications or forms requested by a particular college or program.

☐ Expect most selective colleges to notify your teen-ager in early April of their admissions decision. Some will advise you of their financial aid offer at the same time. Some schools use rolling admission and may notify you sooner or later than April 15.

More than 60 percent of college students in the U.S. receive financial aid!

Glossary

Here's a quick guide to some of the most common abbreviations and terms you may come across when applying to college.

ACT (American College Testing Program Assessment) A standardized test measuring competence in English, mathematics, reading, and science reasoning.

Admissions folder A file kept at a college to which you apply, containing your completed application, high school transcript, standardized test scores, teacher recommendations, and other pertinent information (writing samples, portfolios, and so on).

Admissions Testing Program A testing program administered by the College Entrance Examination Board (CEEB), which includes the SAT I and SAT II.

Advanced Placement (AP) test A test usually given at the end of your junior or senior year, after you have completed certain AP or Honors courses. Many colleges give advanced standing and/or credit for these College Entrance Examination Board (CEEB) sponsored tests.

Advanced standing Some colleges allow students to enter college at the sophomore level, depending on the number of AP courses taken and the scores achieved on the AP tests.

Associate's degree A degree granted by a college or university for a program that requires two years of full-time study.

Award letter The document issued to you by the financial aid office indicating the types, amount, and disbursement dates of the funds awarded from the various financial aid programs, and the conditions that govern the award.

Campus-based financial aid programs Programs administered directly by the college, such as the Federal Work-Study Program.

Candidate's Reply Date Agreement (CRDA) Allows you to defer attendance decisions at participating colleges until

May 1. This enables you to hear from most of the colleges you have applied to before having to select one.

CEEB number An identification number given by the College Board to every high school in the U.S. This number is requested on many college application forms. Check with your guidance office to find your high school's CEEB number and record it in your "personal data portfolio."

Class rank Your standing in your class based on grade point average (GPA). Some schools use percentiles (e.g., top 10%, top 50%); others use rank order (e.g., 10th out of 293).

College Board An independent group that oversees testing and scholarship applications.

College fair A regional or local event where representatives from college admissions offices are present to hand out information and answer your questions.

College-Level Examination Program (CLEP) Provides an opportunity for students (typically adult students) to demonstrate and receive college credit for competency obtained through life experiences. The test consists of five general examinations, with an additional few covering specific subject matter. Some colleges grant credit to students who excel in the exam.

Common Application A generic application accepted by a growing number of colleges and universities.

Cooperative Education (Co-op) A program integrating a classroom study and work experience, offering credit and salary.

Cooperative work-study education Provides full-time paid employment related to a student's field of study. You alternate between work and full-time study. In most cases, a bachelor's program usually takes about five years to complete.

Cost of education Generally, this includes the college tuition and fees as well as the cost of room and board, books and supplies, and transportation expenses.

Deferred entrance An admissions plan that allows an accepted student to postpone entrance for one or more years.

Dependent student A student who is dependent upon his or her parents or legal guardian for financial support or who does not meet the criteria for classification as an independent student.

Early action/early notification An admissions plan that allows you to apply before the normal deadline and receive the college's decision in advance of regular applicants. If you are admitted on this plan, you do not have to accept until May 1 and may still apply to other colleges.

Early decision An admissions plan that allows you to apply before the normal deadline (usually in November or December) and receive the college's decision within a short time. If you are accepted on this plan, you are obligated to enroll at the college and must withdraw any other applications.

Expected Family Contribution (EFC) Amount that you and your parent(s) or legal guardian(s) can reasonably be expected to pay for college.

Federal Work-Study Program An award of part-time employment for students who demonstrate financial need. The maximum amount you can earn under this program is determined by financial need.

Fee waiver Students who can show substantial finan-cial need may be permitted to submit college applica-tions and test registration forms without the typical fee. Check with your guidance counselor for details.

Financial aid package The combination of financial aid that a college awards to a student generally from federal and state grants, scholarships, student loans, and/or work-study jobs.

Free Application for Federal Student Aid (FAFSA) The U.S. Department of Education form required to apply for all federal financial aid, and many state, private, and institutional funds as well. Forms are available at high school guidance offices, local libraries, and college admissions and financial aid offices.

Grade point average (GPA) Your accumulated academic average based on grades and credits, usually figured on an A = 4.0 scale.

National Association of Intercollegiate Athletics (NAIA)
An athletic governing body to which approxi-mately 500 small four-year colleges and universities belong. The NAIA governs athletic recruitment and scholarship awarding policies.

National Collegiate Athletic Association (NCAA)
An athletic governing body to which 800 colleges and universities belong. Each school chooses a general division I, II, or III and is required to follow the policies regarding recruitment and scholarship awards that have been established for that division.

National Merit Scholarship Qualifying Test (NMSQT)
Scores from the PSAT given in October are used to
determine if a student qualifies for a National Merit
Scholarship.

NCAA Clearinghouse If you are planning to enroll in
college as a freshman and participate in Division I or II
athletics, you must be certified by the NCAA Initial-
Eligibility Clearinghouse. The Clearinghouse ensures
consistent application of NCAA initial-eligibility requirements for all prospective student athletes at all member
institutions.

Needs analysis The process used to evaluate your
financial situation to determine how much financial aid
you need to help meet educational expenses.

Open admissions Anyone can send in an application;
there are no minimum admissions requirements (such as
test scores, class rank, or GPA).

Parents' contribution The part of the Expected Family
Contribution that parents are expected to provide
according to the needs analysis.

PLAN (formerly PACT) Preliminary American College
Program Assessment Test. An assessment program
designed for sophomores, which includes tests in

writing skills, mathematics, reading, and science reasoning, and also contains an interest inventory and study skills assessment.

Preliminary SAT (PSAT) This is an abbreviated form of the SAT I and is designed to give sophomores or juniors an opportunity to practice taking a test that is similar to but shorter (1 hour) than the SAT I. It is given in October of the sophomore or junior year.

PROFILE form or CSS/Financial Aid PROFILE form
A supplemental application form from the College Scholarship Service (CSS)—the financial aid division of the College Board—used by some state and private colleges. Always check with the college financial aid office to request required forms.

Rank in class A rating used to compare one student's academic performance with that of all other students at the same grade level in a given school.

Re-centering A change in the calculation of PSAT and SAT scores, put into effect during the 1994-95 academic year, which raises the average score in the math and verbal sections to 500, with a combined average score of 1000.

Recommendations Letters supporting you written by teachers or counselors and submitted to colleges. Try to choose people who know you very well and who will submit a positive, well-written letter.

Registrar College official who registers students and collects fees. The registrar may also be responsible for keeping permanent records, maintaining student files, and forwarding copies of student transcripts to employers and schools.

Regular decision Most colleges have an early winter application. Students must have applications completed by the college deadline (typically due before February 1). The college will notify applicants by April 15. You then must respond prior to its deadline.

Reserve Officer Training Corps (ROTC) Combines military education with college study leading to a bachelor's degree. Students who commit themselves to future service in the Army, Navy, or Air Force usually are eligible for financial assistance opportunities.

Rolling admission An admissions plan that accepts and acts upon applications throughout the year. Decisions are usually made as soon as your admissions folder is complete.

SAT I: Reasoning Test This three-hour reasoning test measures a student's mathematical and verbal abilities.

SAT II: Subject Test One-hour tests offered in subjects such as English, foreign languages, science, history, and mathematics. These tests measure a student's knowledge of particular subject areas.

Scholarship A form of financial assistance that does not require repayment and is usually made to a student who shows potential for distinction in academic or athletic performance.

Student Aid Report (SAR) The U.S. Department of Education report on your Expected Family Contribution to college costs. The SAR is issued in response to your Free Application for Federal Student Aid (FAFSA), after a standard federal formula determines how much a student and family can contribute to a year of education costs.

Test of English as a Foreign Language (TOEFL) Helps foreign students demonstrate their ability to understand the English language. Many colleges require foreign students to take this test as a routine part of the application process.

Wait list A reserve list used by colleges when students meet the requirements for admission but there is not enough room in a class. A college selects students from this list if room becomes available.

Resources

Books

Peterson's Guide to Four-Year Colleges
Peterson's
2000 Lenox Drive, 3rd Floor
Lawrenceville, NJ 08648
609-896-1800

Peterson's Guide to Two-Year Colleges
Peterson's
2000 Lenox Drive, 3rd Floor
Lawrenceville, NJ 08648
609-896-1800

The College Handbook
The College Board
45 Columbus Avenue
New York, NY 10023-6992
At most bookstores

Web sites

Peterson's Education & Career Center
www.petersons.com

The College Board
www.collegeboard.com

CollegeNET
www.collegenet.com

FAFSA on the Web
www.fafsa.ed.gov

The Student Guide
www.ed.gov./prog_info/SFA

students.gov (student gateway to the U.S. government)
students.gov

There is a lot to think about when applying to college. But the college selection process can be an exciting time! Remember, the earlier you begin planning, the better prepared you'll be. And turn to your parents, teachers, counselors, and friends for support.

This guide was created as part of the LifeWorks® employee resource program, a service of Ceridian Corporation. The LifeWorks program offers expert counseling, local and national referrals, and practical information on a wide range of work, personal, and family issues. Until now, LifeWorks publications have been available only to eligible employees or members. Perseus Publishing is making selected LifeWorks publications available to the public in book form for the first time.

Casey Watts is a writer and editor at Ceridian. She has written extensively on parenting topics with a focus on teenagers. A number of LifeWorks education experts contributed to this book.